The poet asks the world to "turn another day" so he can wake up once again by his loved one's side. She is his "New Mexico compass" and her love his "daily bread." The model for these love poems he tells us is Neruda's "*Twenty Love Poems and A Song of Despair.*" Bill Greenwood has given us his 20 love poems and left the "Song of Despair" for someone else to write. His ending is "A Song of Hope." Good choice. Reader, enjoy.

—Nils Peterson, *Poet Laureate Emeritus,* Santa Clara County, author of *Comedy of Desire* and *A Walk to the Center of Things*

In *Twenty Love Poems and A Song of Hope*, Greenwood speaks to us of love that impresses as both personal and universal in tone. Foregoing any operatic endings of tragedy and loss, the poems, filled with the language of music—*largo, pianissimo* and more—deliver the candle-warm ambience of long-term, and sometimes lusty, love. From the opening poem dedication with its wish that "these artesian words come buoy you wrapped in the angel's wings…" to the intimacies of a shared bed where "I ballet point a right foot into the sheets…" to keep from waking his partner, to the imaginings of a final farewell should one mate die before the other, the poems deliver a full-throated celebration that can lead nowhere but to a "Song of Hope" for more time to enjoy the bliss real love can bring. What does the world need now? *Twenty Love Poems and A Song of Hope*.

—Katherine Hastings, *Poet Laureate Emerita*, Sonoma County, author of *Cloud Fire* and *A Different Beauty*

Twenty Love Poems and A Song of Hope presents us with three Wonders. First, that compared to the normal wanderings of a human soul, William Greenwood spent more than thirty years in the middle of his life pursuing a straight path. Second, that from myriad particolored influences, Shakespeare to Neruda, Roethke to Oppen, this poet wove one golden thread. And finally, he sings the highest and rarest note a man can sing, a meticulously refined adoration of his wife.

—Chris Biffle, author of *Whole Brain Teaching* and *Garden in the Snowy Mountains*

twenty love poems
and
a song of hope

WILLIAM GREENWOOD

GREEN HORSE PRESS

First Edition copyright © 2024 by William Greenwood

All rights reserved. No part of this book may be reproduced in any manner without written permission from the publisher, except in brief quotations used in articles or reviews.

ISBN 978-0-931552-29-8

All poems are previously unpublished.

Book design by the author.
The cover artwork is by Paul Widess, used by permission.

The author extends his gratitude to Sandra Anfang, Terry Ehret and Chris Biffle for comments on earlier versions of some of these poems. And to Bill Vartnaw, Taurean Horn Press, for his assistance on the technical process of publication.

Direct all inquiries to:
william.greenwood@gmail.com
Green Horse Press
380 Jewell Avenue
Sebastopol CA 95472

Green Horse Press
is an imprint of Taurean Horn Press
P. O. Box 526
Petaluma, CA 94952-0526

Printed in the United States of America

Not from the stars do I my judgment pluck,
And yet methinks I have astronomy—
But not to tell of good or evil luck,
Of plagues, of dearths, or seasons' quality;
Nor can I fortune to brief minutes tell,
Pointing to each his thunder, rain, and wind,
Or say with princes if it shall go well
By oft predict that I in heaven find.
But from thine eyes my knowledge I derive
And constant stars, in them I read such art
As truth and beauty shall together thrive....

from Sonnet XIV
by William Shakespeare

CONTENTS

Dedication	1
Yes and No Tsunami	2
Spontaneous Combustion	3
The Bather in Question	4
Proof at the Outer Banks	5
Yours Is the Body	6
Pledge	7
Bifocal Vision	8
La Mattina	9
Coming To Bed After You	10
Orchestration	11
Genie in the Garden	12
New Mexico Compass	13
Caribbean Listing	14
A Tall Island Tale	15
Volcano, Hawaii 96785	16
Octopus Love	17
Purse Seiner	18
Terrestrial Hello	19
Knowing When	20
A Song of Hope	21
Notes	24
Afterword	26
Author	28

to Sylvia

Twenty Love Poems and A Song of Hope

DEDICATION

May these artesian
words come buoy you
wrapped in the angel's
wings that brought me
straight to your heart
from mine of which
now you cannot escape
like light from the universe

once   set   free.

Yes and No Tsunami

I drove out on the wharf
the middle of a Friday as agreed,
no matter that the February clouds
weighed in like concrete blocks.

The worn planks rumbled
under my slow wheels
until, once inside, I grabbed
a table by the picture window,
watched the water roll and
searched the bay for gumption.

Who knows what we had to eat
—lunch lasted into dinner.
No tsunamis hit the coast
that afternoon, but my Richter
seismographic kept on
going off the charts.

SPONTANEOUS COMBUSTION

We made our way
across a meadow.
Wind blew through
tall grass like water.

Wild iris tightly
hugged the ground
beneath the waves.

My fingers kayaked
fjords between yours,

circling your wrist,
coursing a full arm's
length to skirt this
brand new continent.

My braille tongue
moved the way
the sea does
with the shore,

then contradicted
all the laws of physics
and combusted.

THE BATHER IN QUESTION

Leaning forward, cantilevered
into mirrored light

as if about to dive,
your stirring wakes me.

Arched across your back,
a French blue towel

slowly sliding falls
down to the floor.

My eyes come to rest
and eddy, echoing

the pears of your body,
the shape of my answer.

PROOF AT THE OUTER BANKS

Boa tight, your contours mirror
this bronze and this copper
and blood-orange sand.

Your pulse connects
the spiraled cochlea
inside my inner ear
to the fact of your heart.

I offer this circuitous
proof of our love.

A pelican pulls one steady wing
apart from the other

and back
          together
again.

Yours Is the Body

Yours is the body I want
to spend the night beside.

Yours are the arms
I can't wait to unfold
reaching left and right
from those shoulders to die for.

Yours are the very legs
this torso longs to feel
wrapped all the way
around my humble corpus.

And your almost liquid
skin is the one earthly surface
I yearn to wake up to.

PLEDGE

My eyes wide
to read your every line,
my cascading sight to deciphering
your body language.

My spooner hands
to your offering shoulders,
the arc of your arm's
sweet lock keyed to mine.

My prehensile feet
to wander like moccasins
the length of your legs
under cover of night.

And my lips undumbfounding
to your love, my daily bread,
your whole wheat baking
in the fires of my heart.

BIFOCAL VISION

The new day comes into view
beyond the upstairs window
that familiar limbs sidelong across.

A light breeze reveals
itself throughout the leaves,
a whole world away from the roots.

Inside our second story,
my hands with their following arms
go looking for you.

As the wind picks up,
our trunks branch together
for the coming storm.

La Mattina

Geraniums erupted green to red
across verandas under the Italian sun
when we spilled the breakfast
pitcher full of *maracuya*.

Bright orange juice
pooled across the terra cotta tiles—
its reflection bouncing up onto the ceiling
of our whitewashed room.

That spot light flickered
like the leaves of morning glory
trailing from the pergola, stitching
the clouds to the horizon.

Such a visual adagio echoed
the promise we would last
for as long as the aquamarine
maneuvers with the deep blue sea.

Coming to Bed After You

Hands first in the dark: wall,
waall…cooorner…jambb…
through thin air to bed
where you breathe *sotto voce*.

Slipping out of my things, I ballet
point a right foot into the sheets,

shifting my weight off the left,
largo, largo, wincing

so no sharps or flats can sound
to puncture your dream,
then, *pianissimo*, I settle in.

My percussion slows
until your sleeping body
spoons back to mine.

ORCHESTRATION

Kettle drums boom in
the beginning of time
for the full orchestra.

Strings vibrate story lines
reverberating inside
these most convex bodies.

Alloyed brass horns'
valves and slides
herald an absolute sunlight.

And woodwinds channel
airs across the reeds
as I work keys

to unlock our concerto.

Genie in the Garden

When you pass
along the back walk,
the heirloom rose hips
stir in your wake
on top of their canes.

Your savory oregano
and fingerling thyme
unleash themselves
in my olfactory brain.

I stop at the lemon tree
plucking one out
from under the sun.

Rubbed in my hands,
it begins to slip,
to shine, exuding
essential oil.

NEW MEXICO COMPASS

When no birds arrive to announce jasper dawn,
you orient the mystery out of the east.

When my feet stutter under cactus sun,
you turn the sky turquoise and bring the south home.

When the flint of the day no longer sparks,
you stand for the sunset off in the west.

And when the bark of not one tree bears moss
all the obsidian night, you are my north.

Caribbean Listing

We float on blue trade winds
suspended by the hammock strings
of our good fortune.

A coco palm curves into backdrop sky.
Canary yellow goldfinch effervesce
about the crown's inverted basket
of lime-colored fruit.

Green fronds clack
their herringbone fingers.

A hummingbird rustles
the passionflower vine.

I starboard list
alongside your port.

As we tie up,
flying fish set sail.

A Tall Island Tale

Once upon a time, two fish flew away and landed on a beach of coral sand named *Agua Dulce*, Sweet Water.

From a nearby perch, an old scarlet macaw squinted his one good eye and parroted how the surrounding sea had seven shades of blue.

Our two grounded mates wasted no time before they put down roots. And coming into flower, they rivaled local orchids.

To this day the native islanders all swear nary a pirate, not a single buccaneer, has ever gotten any richer than these three-cornered lovers—heart, body and soul.

Volcano, Hawaii 96785

We didn't get roped in
and burned by the hot hands
pahoehoe lava roiled out
from under the Big Island's skin,

nor see it come alive,
although we walked across
its next of kin, *a'-a'*,
quasi broken glass.

Clouds peeled back stars
as we climbed to a room
in myrtle trees, *ohia lehua*,
named for ancient lovers.

Come morning, *apapane*
honey creepers sang,
and my fingers ukuleled
your topography awake.

Octopus Love

When we leave the vertical
world behind
                and slide between
sheets of cool water,

our twosome
                reconfigures arms
with legs to eight
                invertebrate
limbs made of muscle.

Elastically they wrap
                each other,
flexing and reflexing
until we snap
                into place.

Firing neurons synapse
in our suction-cupping skin,

and everything we think
imprints in colored ink.

PURSE SEINER

Into the worlds we are
apart for weeks on end,

my empty-handed longing
seines the open sea,

a bottomless net.

But no matter the distance
from the lute in my mind
to your piano hands,

my two fold each other
in an act of prayer

where I purse lone words,

nurturing them
into small schools of thought,

and with these lace
a map to your heart.

TERRESTRIAL HELLO

I cross the equator bound for home
after too many weeks away.

Before my eyes unfold
massive systems of weather

from which you—meteor-
ologically—step center stage,

escort me out to sea
and off to sleep

…. …. ….
"*FASTEN SEAT BELTS!*"

Landing gear clunks to position
pneumatics for asphalt.

Abrupt smoking skid marks
then signal the onset

of my earthbound slowing
to come fully docked

to your safe harbor gate's
now parting lips.

KNOWING WHEN

When my multicolored eyes
are closing on the world
and blacking out, know they never
opened wider than on you.

When my lips are sealed for good
and giving up the ghost, you can tell
whoever's there how when ours met
we rediscovered electricity.

When my hands lose their reach
and they can only hold each other,
remember that my holding yours
was cupping liquid gold.

So when my feet dance their last steps
and my soles leave the floor,
they'll be marking time
with you alone into hereafter.

A Song of Hope

Dawn comes in the kitchen window
bud-break green out of the naked maple.
Steam rises from the wooden fence
like a blessing following the light.

May such good fortune
once again befall me that I see
our round world turn another day
to wake up by your side.

How do I thank the stars
for dropping squarely
in the luck of my two hands
O you apple of these eyes

who from the whorls
of my fingers conjures
lines of praise and
psalms of song.

fin

NOTES

LA MATTINA

The title is Italian for 'the morning'. The word *maracuya* refers to passion fruit (*Passiflora edulis*). Native to the tropics of Latin America, the juice is often marketed in Europe by its name in Portuguese, *maracuja*, as well as the unaccented form of the Spanish word, *maracuyá*.

OUR TALL ISLAND TALE

On the Colombian island of *Providencia* there is a bay named *Agua Dulce*. Like many other Caribbean islands, in the Seventeenth and Eighteenth Centuries it was frequented by British pirates. Today both English and Spanish are spoken there and sometimes used interchangeably in place names; thus the beach in this instance is also called 'Sweet Water'.

VOLCANO, HAWAII 96785

On the Island of Hawaii, just outside the entrance to Kilauea National Park, is the small town of Volcano, ZIP code 96785. The island was created by volcanic activity, so old lava flows are evident, especially throughout the southern part of the island. The quality of these are differentiated by their Hawaiian names, either 'smooth' lava, *pahoehoe*, often described as 'ropey'; or 'sharp' lava, *a'-a'*, which is indeed razor sharp.

A large evergreen species of flowering myrtle, *ohia lehua* (*Metrosideros polymorpha*) is the state tree. It commonly grows to a height of 75 feet or more, and is strong enough that a stand of them could support the tree house where we lodged. The *apapane* is a small, crimson-colored songbird in the honey creeper family. It too is endemic to Hawaii.

Afterword

The first February after we married, I went shopping to find a Valentine card for my wife. But work had taken us to the Middle East where, alas, the day is not celebrated. After several hours of unsuccessful searching, thus obliged to make one myself, I wrote my wife a love poem. It worked to good effect so when her birthday rolled around, I wrote her another one. I mused that in a couple of decades she just might have inspired the equivalent of Neruda's *Twenty Love Poems*.

This had been the first book I ever read that made me truly grateful for learning Spanish. Here were lines so concrete and direct they could have been spoken by one of the Mexican farm laborers I had worked with back home:

> *Quiero hacer contigo lo que la primavera hace con los cerezos.*
>
> I want to do with you what spring does with the cherry trees.

Such lines had the exuberance of a young man's first love spoken with naïve truth and uncommon beauty. And

Neruda's work contained the first poems I attempted to translate into English. Yet, despite their simplicity, time and again I found their adequate translation stubbornly impossible:

> *Cuerpo de mujer, blancas colinas, muslos blancos,*
> *te pareces al mundo en tu actitud de entrega....*

> Womanly body, white hills, white thighs,
> you look like the world stretched out in surrender....

The full title of Neruda's second book was, *Veinte Poemas de Amor y Una Canción Desesperada* ("Twenty Love Poems and A Song of Despair"). Precocious as Rimbaud, Neruda wrote these poems when he was a teenager. His book has long stood as an ideal in the realm of love poetry. The passion of youth which drives so much of its strength, however, leads in my mind to a corollary weakness—many of the poems do not register for a more deeply-rooted, mature love. Thus it concludes with a flaw, I hazard to think, by ending with love's loss and "... Despair". Wouldn't it be better to end celebrating "... Hope" and its fulfillment? If so, then with respect and humility, I offer this attempt at a corresponding rectification.

WG

Author

William Greenwood was born in Arizona. He studied languages and social sciences, ultimately receiving a degree in philosophy *cum laude* from the University of California.

After joining the farm workers' struggle for justice during early unionization, he organized the first agricultural producer-marketing cooperative of Mexican farm workers. This led to a career in development which took him to residencies in Latin America, the Middle East and Central Asia, working on agricultural and small business projects.

In the 1970's he co-founded Green Horse Press with a small group of poets to translate and publish new poetry previously unavailable to English-speakers. Green Horse published his translation of a selection from Guatemalan poet Arqueles Morales' *La Paz Aún No Ganada* which had been selected for the 1971 Cuban *Colección La Honda*; as well as his first chapbook, *Into the Center of America*.

In 2014 Word Temple Press published *Landscape/Cityscape*, of which Paul Vangelisti wrote: "*Greenwood resumes his singular, sometimes eccentric explorations, getting at the core of what language may propose for one's way of living. It is a sensual, hard-bought knowledge that pervades Greenwood's poetry, founded in and of the world, reinforced by the adventure of language.*" The present chapbook, *Twenty Love Poems and A Song of Hope*, was a finalist one year for the Blue Light Poetry Prize.

Caballo Verde para la Poesía
Green Horse for Poetry
the name of the magazine
edited by Pablo Neruda
in Spain in the 1930's
until the Civil War

www.ingramcontent.com/pod-product-compliance
Lightning Source LLC
Chambersburg PA
CBHW062114290426
44110CB00023B/2809